I0488719

13

Business Ideas
Generating Machines

A Lot of Entrepreneurial & Business
Ideas From Each Machine

Salehe A Nantembelele

Published by:

CreateSpace Independent Publishing Platform

United State of America

ISBN-13: 978-1519534538
ISBN-10: 1519534531

This page intentionally left blank

To three women I love the most;

Rukia, Fatuma & Amne

Table of Content

Introduction

Until you find this book on your hand or personal computer you might have struggling to find the business idea that can change your life. A lot of information on how to get business idea is available in internet and various books but still it takes someone more than a year finding to find the idea to execute. There is a good chances that you may have read even more than 100 pages books about how to get business idea but yet you are searching for more, this is to "certify" that the contents of what you have been reading was either not useful to you and or your environment.

Generating business ideas has become the first and foremost obstacle to starting a business. Most of people are interested in starting and running a business but they stack at the point of finding the business idea they can start with.

1

Here I have highlighted 13 business ideas generating machines that will each give you a lot of starting up business ideas. At minimum, if you get about 5 ideas from each machine you then have more than 50 ideas from which you can choose one to go for.

Some of these machines will give you new business ideas, some traditional business ideas and some will give you both.

Now take a look and try to practise rather than just think about the machines themselves.

Business plan competitions

There are some institutions and companies that tend to promote entrepreneurship by conducting "Business Plan Competition" where by participants are required to prepare a business plan and submit to them. Then they find the best business plan (based on their criteria) and reward the winner.

Most of the time these competitions target a certain group of people especially high school, college or university students or any person under a certain age let say 21.

You can talk to these institutions or their personnel and find out if you can have access to those submitted business plans and just go through executive summaries to find out the business idea that you can work on. Trust me you will find something that you have never dream of before, but expect to find weird ideas as far as the nature of competitions are concerned – don't worry, that is a characteristic of a new idea.

In this way you may find both new and existing ideas. Further more you will have some basics for preparation of your business plan from these plans.

If you use this method to get a business idea please read the caution in the following section *"Existing Business Ideas"* third paragraph in a point named *"Financial Institutions"*.

Bigger perspective

Let you think, look and view small things in your life in a bigger perspective. This is mostly concerned with doing online business. If you can view services offered on the internet you can find out that there are things that either was offered in the real world before evolution internet or they solve a problem that could not be solved before the evolution of internet.

You can just spot little things or usual things around your normal everyday life may be in your room, street, office, school or anywhere and think on how you can turn them to business ideas.

Just think about these websites;

- ✓ *ebay.com*: Let think of it for example, it is like a very large complex "mall" in the real world that would require construction of a complex buildings and need a lot of money to run. But somebody sat down and thought that s/he can convert the idea of a mall, plaza or shopping canter to the internet world where they can run it at a very low cost compare to the real world mall.

- ✓ *amazon.com*: in the real world, it is like a large shop of books located somewhere in the middle of the city with branches in every country. Somebody thought about how selling book can be more effective if they can be found for sell at people's finger tips. He does not need large stores every country to sell books, he just needs software that can enable user to examine the book the same way s/he could do in the real world book shop, to read some information about the book, ask for price, and put it in the shopping cart and finally purchasing the book.

- ✓ *google.com*: What is the real world idea of google.com? Simple, it is a huge library full of references, articles, books and more. Somebody thought about how to make referencing easier as a result of google.com. Furthermore, think about other products of google.com like google drive that act like a shelf in your room where you put all your documents, books, letter and everything.

- ✓ *youtube.com*: If you imagine the real world original idea for youtube.com you will find out that it is like a movie theatre full of movies collection. Somebody found out about movie theatre and turn it to an opportunity online.

- ✓ *facebook.com*: Think about a place where group mates meet just to talk and refresh, it can be under a tree, at city garden, in a house and so on. It is just a meeting not for work purpose but just to talk and pass time. In these meetings mates tend to talk about their lives, appreciate (like), comments, bring stories that they heard from somewhere else (share) or take stories from there to somewhere else. The same thing that we do every day, someone took it as an opportunity and a business idea.

University researches

This is a place for new business ideas; universities tend to conduct researches on various innovations that may improve standards of living for the society at large. Most of the time these researches remain in papers waiting for entrepreneurs to put them in action.

Good thing about these researches is that they have been researched by professionals and contains true facts. You only need to be care about the time passed since the time of research and the time you want to implement. See if there might be significant changes in facts due to the passage of time.

What bothers you?

Is there anything bothering you? Things like those you interact every day? Things in your office, home, college, farm, businesses, car, garden, to your pet, children room, or any where? Do not think very far, just little things that you think they are not proper the way they are now, or they disturb you the way they are now and you wish they should not be the way they are. Those things do not only bother you, there are others too bothered by the same things, and the question is – to what extent?

If it bothers many people and you find a way that can stop it from bothering you then you may have find a new product or service. You just need to find out how you can put your solution in a proper manner and turn it into a business.

Think about these examples. Previous people used their hands to remove some stuffs like meat that stuck between their teeth. Sometimes they used any little stick found nearby as long as they were believed to be clean.

Those stuffs disturbed people and there was no product specific for that purpose. Someone saw it as an opportunity and started to produce tooth stick. If you can witness, now there are billions of tooth sticks exported and imported from one country to another everyday. If you where at that time before could you think about producing little sticks for teeth? If yes, what could be the reaction of your friends if you could ask them for advice?

Another example, little children do cry most of the time and if you want them to stop you have to give them a bottle of milk then they stop. Some time you find that they are not hungry but they just cry for something else, again if you feed them they stop crying.

From this disturbing behaviour of children and the short term solution applied someone thought about the permanent solution by manufacturing a "mouth toy" that can make a child feels like eating something, at the same time it serves other purposes like avoiding putting other unsafe objects in the mouth.

Financial Institutions

When you need a financial support for your business from financial institutions like banks and saving and credit association you will be required to submit your business plan before you can be granted a fund. Due to this procedure financial institutions remains with hundreds of business plans submitted for finance.

Now you may approach these financial institutions or their personnel to find out if you can have access to these plans. Like in the point of "Business Plan Competition" above, you will find some basics for your plan if you successful get one from these financial institutions.

Caution; Let these plans help you generate the business ideas and use them as they are, it is not fare, it is not good for your business and again you might find yourself work on the path used by some failures. If you find a business idea that attracts you among those plans then you should read the whole plan but do not implement it. You will have to follow further steps in this book to bring your business up and running. Remember some people submit business plans to financial institutions for just to meet requirements of getting finance.

Geographical Copy and Paste

What is the scope of your business? Do you want to open a business that will serve just your street and nearby ones like retail shop, barbershop or internet cafe? Do you want to open a business that will serve your region or city like radio station, food delivery service or family doctor? Do you want to open a business that will serve across you country like transportation, manufacturing or insurance company?

If you know the scope of the business you wish to run then you can go beyond your scope and find out what kind of businesses exist there but are not found in your scope. For example, for a street - you may visit other streets far away from your street and observe what they are doing. You may find out that there is a video library out there but there is no one in your area. For a region or city - you may find that there is a famous catering company in their region or city but there is no one in your area. For a country wide scope, just observe what other countries doing, you will find a lot of ideas that does not exist in your area. And in this scope, if you copy an idea that has never exist in your country and bring it at the first place you are regarded as an entrepreneur and that is a "new idea"

Business Directory and Classifieds

Business directory and classifieds are the places where most businesses list their offerings. There are some directories published as books either monthly or annually. Also some magazines and news papers include in their publications mini-directories and classifieds. You may also find a hundreds of business directories and classifieds websites on the internet.

Take a look at those places and you will find some business ideas that you might want to turn into a business. It should not bother you, you will have to take a yellow pages (hard copy) and go through it from the first page to the last one, while going through just note some business ideas that you think you might want to turn into a business. Then you can analyze them one after another and choose what you think will work for you.

Universities' lecturers

University lecturers in entrepreneurship studies every year mark student's assignment or projects on business idea and plan. They are in good position to advice you on a good business idea or give you some students that might help you or even give you some of good business plan he has.

It should be noted that to some lecturers these documents (student's assignments and projects) are confidential, let it be your luck day.

Entrepreneurship Seminars and trainings

Attend entrepreneurship seminars on various subjects concerning entrepreneurship. Regardless what kind of business is discussed you just pay a visit and you may come up with a great idea from it. It is not necessarily that you pay for a seminars or trainings; there are a lot of free seminars online.

The reason for attending these seminars is to see what is inside the kind of business presented. You might not like the idea from the beginning but the seminar may show you the opportunity and a way through to success on that idea.

Not only that, make sure you talk to some people you meet there and make connections, sometime you might find someone with idea but need a partner to execute the idea.

Talk to anonymous

This is some kind of research but it is in a very simple way. Find nearby college, business school, or university that teach business studies especially entrepreneurship. Find the final year students to talk to. You do not need to introduce yourself to the college that you want to talk to their students because it is a personal and friendly discussion.

To be successful you need to be honest and do not lie to them why you are talking to them. Introduce yourself enough and tell them that you are looking for a business idea. You might think that no one will like to give you his idea but no, some will not tell you their ideas and some will tell you and be happy to be asked about what is the best business idea you can go for and why.

You can discuss with them on what business they would like to do when they finish their school and get a capital, or you may direct ask them what business you should go for and why. They are both working.

In all your discussion, take more time and ask more question when you meet someone and his idea interests you. Also take their contacts for future contacts if any.

Target about five to ten interesting ideas and put them in writing.

Twisting existing service or product

You can find the existing business that you think in and have a strong believe that if you twist its features a little it will have an impact in market.

Consider changing the size, colour, packaging, and quality; improve its mobility, accessibility, portability, simplicity in use, safety and performance. Also consider combination with other products or helping accessories and adding some new feature.

You need first to choose the product that has market by itself and doing all those twisting to add value.

Government authorities

There are government bodies, authorities or institutions which deal with supporting promotion of local businesses in the country. These organizations have useful information concerning current business opportunities in term of finance and markets. Find how many they are and visit them to see what you can get from them. Surely, you will get more than that from them.

Talents, Skills, Knowledge, Hobbies and interest

You can assess yourself and see if you have any talents, skills, knowledge or any interest. If you have some then list them down and try to brainstorm and think on how you can use them as a source of good business idea that you can start with.

For example, you might have a good skill in the use of some accounting package software in your office as an accountant, or you understand very well your hotel management software in your office in such a way that when any one has a problem with it he calls you first. If this is so and if you most of the time help your co-workers then you may think of starting accounting package trainer.

For the same example, in a simple manner, you will just have to find the whole syllabus, study it clear and go for the market of your training services. You may include in your service the whole process of purchasing the software for your customers, installing and training.

Another example, you might be some funny person and your friends likes to be with you because you make them laugh most of the time. That is a talent, and you can turn it into a business in a several ways, think what if you find a page or part of a page in a newspaper for your funny stuffs, or what if you go for a TV shows, or just writing some books or start a serious blog for your funny stuffs. Think about it, think about everything in you that you see others appreciate, there might be something in it.

Self Questions That May Lead to Business Ideas

- ✓ What do you or your friends want to buy but can't find?
- ✓ What product in the market you believe that it lack something that could add value to its users. Can you add that missing part to it?
- ✓ Do your hobbies and interests have some of values to others around you?
- ✓ Discuss with others and know what businesses they could start if they get all required resources.
- ✓ Discuss your thoughts with friends and family.
- ✓ Visit events prepared by ministries, college and other institutions with a view of spotting out a business idea.
- ✓ Can you redefine your college business project?
- ✓ See what kind of business has a lot of customers
- ✓ What product do customers buy with no other choice?

About the Author

Salehe A Nantembelele has a good experience in business from doing business including online businesses in the past eight years. Currently he is a president of Yuu Company (group of four business units) and a sole owner of Tanzania Website Design (http://www.tanzaniawebsitedesign.com/).

Salehe A Nantembelele is a former Executive Accountant of Taris Consult (sister company of Health Focus Ltd) where he worked for two years and lead to tremendous improvement in the business operations of the group company.

He has a bachelor of commerce (B.com) specialized in accounting taken from University of Dar Es Salaam Business School (UDBS), Currently He is on the way to pursue Master in Business Administration (MBA).

Salehe A Nantembelele is good speaker with rich contents in enterpreneurship, business and blogging in general. He mostly present in various seminars that he is invited.

Salehe A Nantembelele is in love with Amne S Issa – a girl he married in 2014.

www.ingramcontent.com/pod-product-compliance
Lightning Source LLC
Chambersburg PA
CBHW071604170526
45166CB00004B/1790